48

JIMMIE
JOHNSON

Superstars of
NASCAR

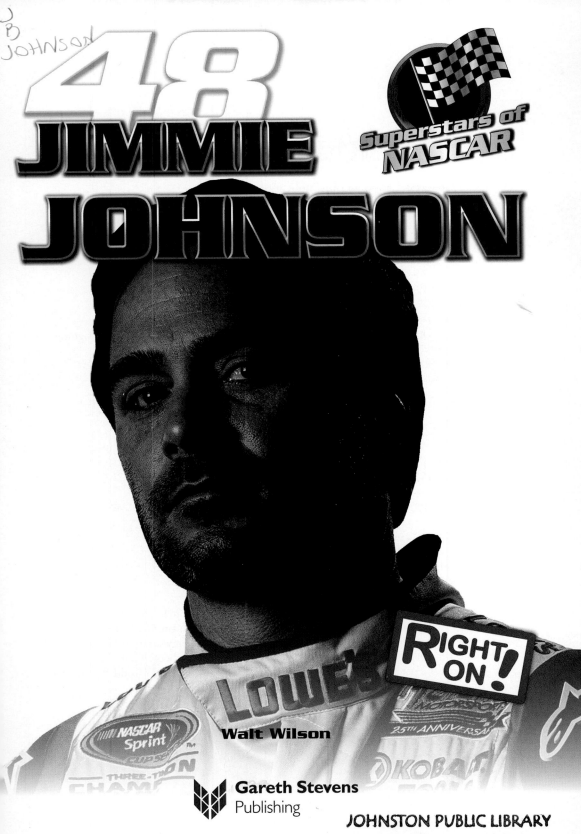

Walt Wilson

Gareth Stevens
Publishing

Please visit our Web site, www.garethstevens.com. For a free color catalog of all our high-quality books, call toll free 1-800-542-2595 or fax 1-877-542-2596.

Library of Congress Cataloging-in-Publication Data

Wilson, Walt.
Jimmie Johnson / Walt Wilson.
    p. cm. — (Superstars of NASCAR)
Includes index.
ISBN 978-1-4339-3957-0 (pbk.)
ISBN 978-1-4339-3958-7 (6-pack))
ISBN 978-1-4339-3956-3 (library binding)
1. Johnson, Jimmie, 1975—Juvenile literature. 2. Stock car drivers--United States—Biography—Juvenile literature. 3. Automobile racing drivers—United States—Biography—Juvenile literature. I. Title.
GV1032.J54W45 2010
796.72092—dc22
[B]
                              2010007389

First Edition

Published in 2011 by
Gareth Stevens Publishing
111 East 14th Street, Suite 349
New York, NY 10003

Copyright © 2011 Gareth Stevens Publishing

Designer: Michael J. Flynn
Editor: Mary Ann Hoffman

Photo credits: Cover (Jimmie Johnson), pp. 1, 19, 25 Rusty Jarrett/Getty Images; cover, pp. 4, 6, 8, 10, 14, 16, 18, 22, 24, 26, 28 (background on all) Shutterstock.com; p. 5 Christian Petersen/Getty Images; pp. 7, 20–21 Jonathan Ferrey/Getty Images; p. 9 Ronald Martinez/Getty Images; pp. 11, 12–13, 15 Robert Laberge/Getty Images; p. 17 Jeff Gross/Getty Images; p. 23 Chris Trotman/Getty Images; p. 27 Todd Warshaw/Getty Images; p. 29 Jeffrey Mayer/WireImage/Getty Images.

Printed in the United States of America

CPSIA compliance information: Batch #CS10GS: For further information contact Gareth Stevens, New York, New York at 1-800-542-2595.

Contents

A Young Racer

Jimmie Johnson was born in California on September 17, 1975. He began racing motorcycles when he was only 5 years old!

When he was a little older, Jimmie raced in off-road races. He raced both cars and trucks.

7

NASCAR

When Jimmie was 22, he began racing on paved tracks. He raced in the ASA Series and in NASCAR's Nationwide Series.

The Cup Series

In 2002, Jimmie moved up to NASCAR's Sprint Cup Series. His first win was at his home track—the Auto Club Speedway in California.

11

Jimmie was very happy about winning in California. He made donuts on the racetrack after the race!

Jimmie won two more Sprint Cup Series races that year. Many people saw what a good driver he was.

In 2003, Jimmie scored the second-highest number of points among NASCAR drivers.

NASCAR
Winston Cup
Series
LOWE'S
POWER OF PRIDE
Jimmie Johnson

Champion in the Making

In 2004, Jimmie won eight races. That was the most races won by any driver that year!

Jimmie Johnson

Jimmie won four races in 2005. He was the only driver to be in the top 10 after every race.

Driver of the Year

Jimmie became the Sprint Cup champion for the first time in 2006. He was voted NASCAR's Driver of the Year, too.

Jimmie won four races in a row in 2007. Not many other drivers have done that! He was Driver of the Year and Sprint Cup champion again.

A Four-Time Champion

Jimmie was Sprint Cup champion in 2008 and 2009. That meant he was champion four years in a row. No other driver in NASCAR history has done that!

A Helping Hand

Jimmie and his wife started the
Jimmie Johnson Foundation in 2006.
They raise money to help children
and schools. They also help families
and communities in need.

Timeline

1975 Jimmie is born in California.

1998 Jimmie begins racing in NASCAR.

2004 Jimmie wins eight races.

2006 Jimmie wins his first Sprint Cup championship.

2006 Jimmie and his wife start the Jimmie Johnson Foundation.

2007 Jimmie wins four races in a row.

2009 Jimmie is Sprint Cup champion for the fourth year in a row.

For More Information

Books:

Doeden, Matt. *Jimmie Johnson*. Mankato, MN: Capstone
    Press, 2009.

Pristash, Nicole. *Jimmie Johnson*. New York, NY: Rosen
    Publishing Group, 2009.

Web Sites:

Hendrick Motorsports: Jimmie Johnson
hendrickmotorsports.com/racing-bio.asp?pers=70&team=4

Jimmie Johnson Foundation
jimmiejohnsonfoundation.org

Glossary

ASA: the American Speed Association, which is an official racing series

champion: a winner

donut: a fast, tight turn in a circle

foundation: a group to raise money for different causes

motorcycle: a sort of bicycle with two wide tires and a motor

off-road: not on a paved road

Sprint Cup Series: the top racing series of NASCAR

Index